To

From

It is God who arms me with strength,

and makes my way perfect.

2 Samuel 22:33

footprints

SCRIPTURE *with* REFLECTIONS

for Teens

INSPIRED *by the* BEST-LOVED POEM

Our Heavenly Father is faithful and will never leave us or forsake us. As we come to him daily, willing to be shaped and directed, his Word gives clear direction. Almost everything we read, see, and experience shows us in some way that, although we do not visibly see God, he is with us. Over centuries of time others have looked back to understand that God's Spirit and presence were there, even when they felt alone.

In our quiet moments of reflection, in the fellowship of others and even in dreams, God opens the doors to our hearts. This is what happened when I originally wrote the poem, "Footprints." After hours of wrestling with the darkness of doubt and despair, I finally surrendered to him and, in the early morning light of peace, wrote the poem as result of that spiritual experience.

Each of us is different in our spiritual need, just as each of our days is different. God wants to place his signature on your life in a unique way. As you spend time, even just a few moments each day, reflecting on his Word, it will help you to know him better.

Margaret Fishback Powers

footprints

One night I dreamed a dream.
I was walking along the beach with my Lord.
Across the dark sky flashed scenes from my life.
For each scene, I noticed two sets of footprints
in the sand,
one belonging to me and one to my Lord.
When the last scene of my life shot before me
I looked back at the footprints in the sand
and to my surprise,
I noticed that many times along the path of my life
there was only one set of footprints.
I realized that this was at the lowest
and saddest times of my life.
This always bothered me
and I questioned the Lord about my dilemma.
"Lord, you told me when I decided to follow You,
You would walk and talk with me all the way.
But I'm aware that during the most troublesome
times of my life there is only one set of footprints.
I just don't understand why, when I needed You most,
You leave me."
He whispered, "My precious child,
I love you and will never leave you
never, ever, during your trials and testings.
When you saw only one set of footprints
it was then that I carried you."

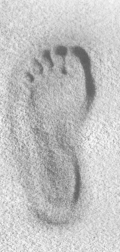

God *is* With Us...

in Our Dreams

One night I dreamed a dream.

The Bible tells us about many people who had dreams and visions that were given to them by God.

God sent dreams to give wisdom and direction, and to test the purity of a man's heart.

At Gibeon the LORD appeared to Solomon during the night in a dream, and God said, "Ask for whatever you want me to give you."

Solomon answered,... "O LORD my God, you have made your servant king in place of my father David. But I am only a little child and do not know how to carry out my duties. Your servant is here among the people you have chosen, a great people, too numerous to count or number. So give your servant a discerning heart to govern your people and to distinguish between right and wrong. For who is able to govern this great people of yours?"

The Lord was pleased that Solomon had asked for this. So God said to him, "Since you have asked for this and not for long life or wealth for yourself, nor have asked for the death of your enemies but for discernment in administering justice, I will do what you have asked. I will give you a wise and discerning heart, so that there will never have been anyone like you, nor will there ever be. Moreover, I will give you what you have not asked for—both riches and honor—so that in your lifetime you will have no equal among kings. And if you walk in my ways and obey my statutes and commands as David your father did, I will give you a long life."

1 Kings 3:5–14

God sent dreams that revealed his plans and protected his people.

This is how the birth of Jesus Christ came about: His mother Mary was pledged to be married to Joseph, but before they came together, she was found to be with child through the Holy Spirit. Because Joseph her husband was a righteous man and did not want to expose her to public disgrace, he had in mind to divorce her quietly.

But after he had considered this, an angel of the Lord appeared to him in a dream and said, "Joseph son of David, do not be afraid to take Mary home as your wife, because what is conceived in her is from the Holy Spirit. She will give birth to a son, and you are to give him the name Jesus, because he will save his people from their sins."

Matthew 1:18–21

An angel of the Lord appeared to Joseph in a dream. "Get up," he said, "take the child and his mother and escape to Egypt. Stay there until I tell you, for Herod is going to search for the child to kill him." So he got up, took the child and his mother during the night and left for Egypt, where he stayed until the death of Herod. And so was fulfilled what the Lord had said through the prophet: "Out of Egypt I called my son."

Matthew 2:13–15

After Herod died, an angel of the Lord appeared in a dream to Joseph in Egypt and said, "Get up, take the child and his mother and go to the land of Israel, for those who were trying to take the child's life are dead." So he got up, took the child and his mother and went to the land of Israel.

Matthew 2:19–21

God reassured those who loved him of his presence through dreams.

The word of the LORD came to Abram in a vision:
  "Do not be afraid, Abram.
  I am your shield, your very great reward."

Genesis 15:1

God spoke to Israel in a vision at night and said, "Jacob! Jacob!"
  "Here I am," he replied.
  "I am God, the God of your father," he said. "Do not be afraid to go down to Egypt, for I will make you into a great nation there. I will go down to Egypt with you, and I will surely bring you back again."

Genesis 46:2–4

One night the Lord spoke to Paul in a vision: "Do not be afraid; keep on speaking, do not be silent. For I am with you, and no one is going to attack and harm you."

Acts 18:9–10

I looked up and there before me was a man dressed in linen, with a belt of the finest gold around his waist. His body was like chrysolite, his face like lightning, his eyes like flaming torches, his arms and legs like the gleam of burnished bronze, and his voice like the sound of a multitude. ...

He said, "Daniel, you who are highly esteemed, consider carefully the words I am about to speak to you, and stand up, for I have now been sent to you." And when he said this to me, I stood up trembling.

Then he continued, "Do not be afraid, Daniel. Since the first day that you set your mind to gain understanding and to humble yourself before your God, your words were heard, and I have come in response to them."

Daniel 10:5–6, 11–12

We should not ignore our dreams. God will sometimes use our dreams to assure us of his promises or to tell us something about himself. And when God does speak to us in dreams, he will also help us understand them.

[Joseph] asked Pharaoh's officials who were in custody with him in his master's house, "Why are your faces so sad today?"

"We both had dreams," they answered, "but there is no one to interpret them."

Then Joseph said to them, "Do not interpretations belong to God? Tell me your dreams."

Genesis 40:7–8

"When a prophet of the Lord is among you,
I reveal myself to him in visions,
I speak to him in dreams," says the Lord.

Numbers 12:6

There is a God in heaven who reveals mysteries.

Daniel 2:28

God's presence with us is a reality. As we dream our dreams with the knowledge that God is with us, we will begin to see things as Christ does and dream dreams inspired by the Holy Spirit that are worth retelling and following.

Our youngest daughter was in the hospital for an operation and she started feeling very frightened toward evening. As I left the room one night, I kissed her forehead and said, "Don't worry dear. God will send his angels to watch over you."

When I arrived the next morning she was sitting up chattering away to a nurse, her face beaming. Later on, the nurse turned to me and said, "Your daughter has quite an imagination. She was describing to me the angels that were sitting on the end of her bed, and told me not to be afraid, and that her operation would go all right." Later, my daughter described that same dream to me ... giving her angels names. Strangely enough, many years later, as a young woman of eighteen, these same angels visited her again after she experienced a serious accident. Surely that was no coincidence!

One of the many names given to Jesus Christ in the Bible is Emmanuel, which means, literally, "God with us." What a promise is contained in that name! In Christ, God made his dwelling place with ordinary human beings, and as he was returning to heaven, Jesus gave his disciples another great promise, "I am with you always, to the very end of the age." That God is there for us whenever we turn to him is no pipe-dream!

It's a dream come true.

Margaret Fishback Powers

God *is* With Us...

in Our Everyday Lives

★
---

*I was walking along the beach
with my Lord.*

Maybe *you think* that God doesn't want to "be bothered" with the details of your everyday life ... stuff like tests, fights with your parents, and struggles with your friends. Well, if you thought that way, you'd be wrong! God is right beside you every moment of every day, and he wants you to talk to him about everything. If you'll do that, you'll find that he will become your very best friend—one that will never let you down.

God has said: "I will live with them and walk among them, and I will be their God, and they will be my people."

2 Corinthians 6:16

"When you pass through the waters,
I will be with you;
and when you pass through the rivers,
they will not sweep over you.
When you walk through the fire,
you will not be burned;
the flames will not set you ablaze,"
says the LORD.

Isaiah 43:2

The LORD your God is with you,
he is mighty to save.
He will take great delight in you,
he will quiet you with his love,
he will rejoice over you with singing.

Zephaniah 3:17

Just as you received Christ Jesus as Lord, continue to live in him, rooted and built up in him, strengthened in the faith as you were taught, and overflowing with thankfulness.

Colossians 2:6–7

Live a life worthy of the Lord ... please him in every way: bearing fruit in every good work, growing in the knowledge of God, ... and joyfully giving thanks to the Father, who has qualified you to share in the inheritance of the saints in the kingdom of light.

Colossians 1:10–12

Let him who walks in the dark,
   who has no light,
trust in the name of the LORD
   and rely on his God.

Isaiah 50:10

Come near to God and he will come near to you.

James 4:8

Those who know your name will trust in you,
   for you, LORD, have never forsaken those
      who seek you.

Psalm 9:10

If we walk in the light, as he is in the light, we have fellowship with one another, and the blood of Jesus, his Son, purifies us from all sin.

1 John 1:7

I am always with you, LORD;
*   you hold me by my right hand.*

Psalm 73:23

Love the LORD your God ... walk in all his ways ... hold fast to him.

Deuteronomy 11:22

The LORD is the everlasting God,
*   the Creator of the ends of the earth.*
He will not grow tired or weary,
*   and his understanding no one can fathom.*
He gives strength to the weary
*   and increases the power of the weak.*
Even youths grow tired and weary,
*   and young men stumble and fall;*
but those who hope in the Lord
*   will renew their strength.*
They will soar on wings like eagles;
*   they will run and not grow weary,*
*   they will walk and not be faint.*

Isaiah 40:28-31

O Lord, you have searched me
  and you know me.
You know when I sit and when I rise;
  you perceive my thoughts from afar.
You discern my going out and my lying down;
  you are familiar with all my ways.
Before a word is on my tongue
  you know it completely, O Lord.
You hem me in—behind and before;
  you have laid your hand upon me.
Such knowledge is too wonderful for me,
  too lofty for me to attain.

Psalm 139:1–6

From the rising of the sun to the place where it sets,
  the name of the Lord is to be praised.

Psalm 113:3

The Lord is with me; I will not be afraid.
  What can man do to me?
The Lord is with me; he is my helper.

Psalm 118:6–7

And I—in righteousness I will see your face;
  when I awake, I will be satisfied with
  seeing your likeness, Lord.

Psalm 17:15

I will exalt you, my God the King;
  I will praise your name for ever and ever.
Every day I will praise you
  and extol your name for ever and ever.
Great is the LORD and most worthy of praise;
  his greatness no one can fathom.

Psalm 145:1–3

Your love is ever before me, LORD,
  and I walk continually in your truth.

Psalm 26:3

Jesus said, "Come to me, all you who are weary and burdened, and I will give you rest. Take my yoke upon you and learn from me, for I am gentle and humble in heart, and you will find rest for your souls. For my yoke is easy and my burden is light."

Matthew 11:28–30

He holds victory in store for the upright,
  he is a shield to those whose walk
  is blameless.

Proverbs 2:7

One thing I ask of the LORD,
  this is what I seek:
that I may dwell in the house of the LORD
  all the days of my life,
to gaze upon the beauty of the LORD
  and to seek him in his temple.

Psalm 27:4

How great is your goodness, LORD,
  which you have stored up for those who fear you,
which you bestow in the sight of men
  on those who take refuge in you.

Psalm 31:19

"I will strengthen you and help you;
  I will uphold you with my righteous right hand,"
  says the LORD.

Isaiah 41:10

I trust in you, O LORD;
  I say, "You are my God."
My times are in your hands.

Psalm 31:14–15

When I was a little girl, I used to pray about everything. If I was climbing a tree and suddenly realized I couldn't get down, I would ask God to help me. If my stomach hurt I would ask God to heal it. If my cat was lost I would ask God to help me find her. And sometimes, I just sat on my swing in the backyard and sang God a song to tell him I loved him.

Then, I grew up. I still prayed, but mostly just for the "big" things—a relative who had cancer or a missionary who was being persecuted. Somewhere between the ages of 10 and 20, I decided that I could handle the "little things" on my own and that God knew I loved him—I didn't need to sit in the backyard and sing anymore.

Recently, though, I've begun to realize that growing up doesn't mean that you stop "bothering" God with little prayers or that you only praise him at church on Sunday. Does a good dad want his child to stop coming to him for advice and love once the child grows up? No!

God never stops wanting to hear from us about every aspect of our lives, and I imagine he is sad when we lose that "childlike faith" we once had and start carrying all our troubles on our own.

So, while we all must grow up, we never have to stop being God's child. I think I'll go into the backyard and sing him a song ... just to say thanks.

Molly Detweiler

God Is *with* Us ...

In the Hard Times

*Across the dark sky flashed scenes
from my life.*

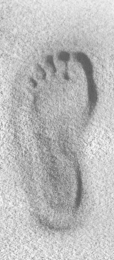

We all go through times when life seems to overwhelm us. The Bible reassures us that God's presence is with us to help us, even when we don't realize it.

God is our refuge and strength,
an ever-present help in trouble.

Psalm 46:1

In my distress I called to the LORD,
and he answered me.
From the depths of the grave I called for help,
and you listened to my cry.

Jonah 2:2

Those who know your name will trust in you,
for you, LORD, have never forsaken
     those who seek you.

Psalm 9:10

You are my hiding place, LORD;
   you will protect me from trouble
   and surround me with songs of deliverance.

Psalm 32:7

Even though I walk
   through the valley of the shadow of death,
I will fear no evil,
   for you are with me, LORD;
your rod and your staff,
   they comfort me.

Psalm 23:4

"Do not fear, for I am with you;
   do not be dismayed, for I am your God."

Isaiah 41:10

God alone is my rock and my salvation;
   he is my fortress, I will never be shaken.

Psalm 62:2

Praise be to the Lord, to God our Savior,
   who daily bears our burdens.

Psalm 68:19

The Lord is my strength and my shield;
my heart trusts in him, and I am helped.

Psalm 28:7

In my distress I called to the LORD;
  I called out to my God.
From his temple he heard my voice;
  my cry came to his ears.

2 Samuel 22:7

God reached down from on high and
    took hold of me;
  he drew me out of deep waters. ...
He brought me out into a spacious place;
  he rescued me because he delighted in me.

2 Samuel 22: 17, 20

Though I have fallen, I will rise.
Though I sit in darkness, the LORD will be my light. ...
He will bring me out into the light;
  I will see his righteousness.

Micah 7:8–9

Because of the tender mercy of our God ...
the rising sun will come to us from heaven
to shine on those living in darkness
and in the shadow of death,
to guide our feet into the path of peace.

Luke 1:78–79

*A righteous man may have many troubles,
  but the LORD delivers him from them all.*

Psalm 34:19

*Jesus said, "In this world you will have trouble. But
take heart! I have overcome the world."*

John 16:33

*Though I walk in the midst of trouble,
  you preserve my life ...
with your right hand you save me, O LORD.*

Psalm 138:7

*The LORD will keep you from all harm—
  he will watch over your life;
the LORD will watch over your coming and going
  both now and forevermore.*

Psalm 121:7-8

A friend of mine, the chaplain of a college, was brokenhearted when he found out one of his brightest students, a Christian, had been hit by a bus and killed. One upset student asked my friend, "Why did Jesus kill Cliff?" My friend answered, "You're an intelligent person. You ought to be able to tell the difference between Jesus and a bus!"

While God doesn't make bad things happen, the Bible promises us that in the midst of bad things, God works to bring good out of it all (see Romans 8:28). There used to be a guy who had his own TV show. And one of the other guys on the show, José Melos, was a fantastic piano player. Sometimes the show host would walk over to the piano and slap his hands down on a bunch of keys. They made an awful sound, of course. Then he would say, "OK, José, let's see what you can make out of that mess!"

José would then put his fingers on the exact keys the show host had played and build those sounds into a magnificent melody. Incredibly, the clashing sounds became a beautiful song.

God can do that with the messes in our lives. God is able to take our tragedies, and the mistakes we make, and turn them into something beautiful.

Tony Campolo

God Is *with* Us ...

As Our Companion

For each scene, I noticed two sets of footprints in the sand, one belonging to me and one to my Lord.

F riends are great. They laugh with us and cry with us. We have more fun just sitting around doing nothing with them than doing something really cool alone.

Two are better than one,
because they have a good return for their work:
If one falls down,
his friend can help him up.
But pity the man who falls
and has no one to help him up!

Ecclesiastes 4:9–10

A friend loves at all times.

Proverbs 17:17

There is a friend who sticks closer than a brother.

Proverbs 18:24

The pleasantness of one's friend springs from his earnest counsel.

Proverbs 27:9

It's pretty amazing when you realize that God wants to be friends with you. He wants to laugh and cry with you. He wants to just sit around and be with you. He actually made you because he wanted to have you as his friend!

God said, "Let us make man in our image, in our like-
ness, and let them rule over the fish of the sea and the
birds of the air, over the livestock, over all the earth, and
over all the creatures that move along the ground."

So God created man in his own image,
in the image of God he created him;
male and female he created them.

Genesis 1:26–27

"I am with you and will watch over you wherever you
go. ... I will not leave you until I have done what I have
promised you," says the LORD.

Genesis 28:15

Jesus said, "Love each other as I have loved you.
Greater love has no one than this, that he lay down his
life for his friends. You are my friends if you do what I
command. I no longer call you servants, because a ser-
vant does not know his master's business. Instead, I
have called you friends, for everything that I learned
from my Father I have made known to you."

John 15:12–15

Even if all your other friends ditch you, God never will. He'll walk with you all the way. You can count on that.

Who shall separate us from the love of Christ? Shall trouble or hardship or persecution or famine or nakedness or danger or sword? ... No, in all these things we are more than conquerors through him who loved us. For I am convinced that neither death nor life, neither angels nor demons, neither the present nor the future, nor any powers, neither height nor depth, nor anything else in all creation, will be able to separate us from the love of God that is in Christ Jesus our LORD.

Romans 8:35, 37–39

The LORD himself goes before you and will be with you; he will never leave you nor forsake you.

Deuteronomy 31:8

"Though the mountains be shaken
 and the hills be removed,
yet my unfailing love for you will not be shaken
 nor my covenant of peace be removed,"
 says the LORD, who has compassion on you.

Isaiah 54:10

God has said,
 Never will I leave you;
 never will I forsake you."

Hebrews 13:5

One of the greatest things about being friends with God is that he's always there and always ready to listen. All you have to do is call and he's all ears, ready and willing to help you and love you.

In my distress I called to the LORD;
I cried to my God for help.
From his temple he heard my voice;
my cry came before him, into his ears.

Psalm 18:6

God has surely listened
and heard my voice in prayer.
Praise be to God,
who has not rejected my prayer
or withheld his love from me!

Psalm 66:19–20

O LORD my God, I called to you for help
and you healed me.

Psalm 30:2

The LORD longs to be gracious to you;
he rises to show you compassion.

Isaiah 30:18

God isn't just your friend for this life. He wants you to be with him for all eternity. And he's planning an incredible place for you to come home to where you can truly be friends forever!

"No eye has seen,
  no ear has heard,
  no mind has conceived
  what God has prepared for those who love him."

1 Corinthians 2:9

The wall of the city had twelve foundations, and on them were the names of the twelve apostles of the Lamb. ... The wall was made of jasper, and the city of pure gold, as pure as glass. The foundations of the city walls were decorated with every kind of precious stone. The first foundation was jasper, the second sapphire, the third chalcedony, the fourth emerald, the fifth sardonyx, the sixth carnelian, the seventh chrysolite, the eighth beryl, the ninth topaz, the tenth chrysoprase, the eleventh jacinth, and the twelfth amethyst. The twelve gates were twelve pearls, each gate made of a single pearl. The great street of the city was of pure gold, like transparent glass.

I did not see a temple in the city, because the Lord God Almighty and the Lamb are its temple. The city does not need the sun or the moon to shine on it, for the glory of God gives it light, and the Lamb is its lamp. The nations will walk by its light, and the kings of the earth will bring their splendor into it

Revelation 21:14, 18–24

Have you ever wondered why God made you or why he made people at all? Well, it wasn't because he needed us. Acts 17:25 says, "[God] ... is not served by human hands, as if he needed anything."

And he didn't make us because he was lonely. Long before we were here, God the Father already had "company" with his Son and the Holy Spirit. All of God's needs for companionship are met within the Trinity. He also didn't make us because he needed people to tell him how great he is. God is totally secure in who he is—and he always has been.

Despite not needing us, God chose to create us anyway, out of his great love. Yes, God loved us before he even created us. This concept is bigger than our tiny brains, but it's true; that's what "everlasting" love means. God is love (see 1 John 4:8), and because of that love and his wonderful creativity, he made us so we can enjoy all that he is and all that he's done.

Because of the deep love God has for you, you will always have at least one unfailing friend! Maybe he's not flesh and blood and waiting at your locker for you after class. But that's part of what's so cool about God. He's a friend who is with you all the time. Whether you're at the cool kid's party or just at home alone, God is always right there with you. The God of the universe is just waiting to spend time with you. Hey, have a blast hanging out with him today!

Dawson McAllister

God Is *with* Us ...

No Regrets!

When the last scene of my life shot before me I looked back at the footprints in the sand.

G *od is the God of grace.* He is the God of hope. He is the God of love who offers us a life free of regrets.

You are a forgiving God, gracious and compassionate, slow to anger and abounding in love.

Nehemiah 9:17

The LORD your God is gracious and compassionate. He will not turn his face from you if you return to him.

2 Chronicles 30:9

Find rest, O my soul, in God alone;
my hope comes from him.
He alone is my rock and my salvation;
he is my fortress, I will not be shaken.

Psalm 62:5–6

The LORD is gracious and righteous;
our God is full of compassion.

Psalm 116:5

We have put our hope in the living God, who is the Savior of all men, and especially of those who believe.

1 Timothy 4:10

Do the skies themselves send down showers?
No, it is you, O LORD our God.
Therefore our hope is in you,
for you are the one who does all this.

Jeremiah 14:22

God is able to make all grace abound to you, so that in all things at all times, having all that you need, you will abound in every good work.

2 Corinthians 9:8

Through Christ you believe in God, who raised him from the dead and glorified him, and so your faith and hope are in God.

1 Peter 1:21

This is love: not that we loved God, but that he loved us and sent his Son as an atoning sacrifice for our sins.

1 John 4:10

Whenever we do look back over our lives we must do so with God's perspective—no remorse or regrets. With God's perspective, we will be able to trace his hand on our lives and see that he has swept up the bad things of life and transformed them to good, just as he promised he would. With God's perspective, we will be able to live above regrets and live in God's peace and joy.

We know that in all things God works for the good of those who love him, who have been called according to his purpose.

Romans 8:28

Blessed is the man who perseveres under trial, because when he has stood the test, he will receive the crown of life that God has promised to those who love him.

James 1:12

We also rejoice in our sufferings, because we know that suffering produces perseverance; perseverance, character; and character, hope. And hope does not disappoint us, because God has poured out his love into our hearts by the Holy Spirit, whom he has given us.

Romans 5:3–5

Dear friends, do not be surprised at the painful trial you are suffering, as though something strange were happening to you. But rejoice that you participate in the sufferings of Christ, so that you may be overjoyed when his glory is revealed. If you are insulted because of the name of Christ, you are blessed, for the Spirit of glory and of God rests on you.

1 Peter 4:12–1

We do not need to live a life of regrets. God doesn't look back over our past and throw our sins back in our face, so why should we do it to ourselves? Once we have confessed and asked for forgiveness, it is done. God doesn't remember our sins and sees us as clean and new. Ask him to help you see yourself as he does!

I acknowledged my sin to you
and did not cover up my iniquity.
I said, "I will confess
my transgressions to the Lord"—
and you forgave
the guilt of my sin.

Psalm 32:5

If we confess our sins, God is faithful and just and will forgive us our sins and purify us from all unrighteousness.

1 John 1:9

As high as the heavens are above the earth,
so great is God's love for those who fear him;
as far as the east is from the west,
so far has he removed our transgressions from us.

Psalm 103:11–12

*"I, even I, am he who blots out
your transgressions, for my own sake,
and remembers your sins no more," says the L*ORD*.*

Isaiah 43:25

*Jesus said, "Be merciful, just as your Father is merciful.
Do not judge, and you will not be judged. Do not con-
demn, and you will not be condemned. Forgive, and you
will be forgiven.*

Luke 6:36--37

*If anyone is in Christ, he is a new creation; the old has
gone, the new has come!*

2 Corinthians 5:17

*Be kind and compassionate to one another, forgiving
each other, just as in Christ God forgave you.*

Ephesians 4:32

*I will sprinkle clean water on you, and you will be clean;
I will cleanse you from all your impurities and from all
your idols. I will give you a new heart and put a new
spirit in you; I will remove from you your heart of stone
and give you a heart of flesh.*

Ezekiel 36:25-26

Let's imagine that you are invited to play in a best-ball golf tournament. That means that if you're paired with someone like Tiger Woods, you will probably win, even if you've never golfed a day in your life!

You tee off for the first shot and shank it about 10 feet off to the right. Woods nails it down the fairway and puts it about 10 feet from the green. Guess what? You get to hit his placement.

You drive it over the green into the creek. Woods plops it up on the green, three feet away from a birdie. Guess what? You get to play that shot.

You bounce it past the green, and it rolls into the rough grass on the edge. Woods taps it in.

Guess what? You get a birdie!

You could go through all 18 holes, slapping balls off trees, knocking others into the water, losing still others in the woods. Yet instead of writing down a big 125 on the scorecard, you get to write down a mind-blowing 68. You get credit for Woods' goodness.

In life, we try to be good, but we keep hitting life's tee shots the wrong way. We chip into trouble. We drive into rough spots. Yet if we have placed our faith in Jesus, the one true Savior, none of it is held against us. The scorecard says, "Forgiven."

And what's even better is that Jesus doesn't have to keep teeing up for us. He made one sacrifice that corrects our record for all time. "Their sins and lawless acts I will remember no more," God says (Hebrews 10:17).

It would be great to play a little best-ball with Tiger Woods, but it's nothing compared to the once-for-all act of Jesus, which makes our record sinless and perfect in God's eyes. No regrets!

The Sports Devotional Bible

God Is *with* Us ...

In Our Loneliness

And to my surprise, I noticed that many times along the path of my life there was only one set of footprints.

B *eing a teen can* be a lonely time. Lots of things are changing and sometimes you feel like no one really understands. When you're feeling lonely, it's good to remember that you aren't the only one who feels this way. Both Jesus and the writer of Psalms knew what it was to feel alone, abandoned, and forgotten.

About the ninth hour Jesus cried out in a loud voice, "Eloi, Eloi, lama sabachthani?"—which means, "My God, my God, why have you forsaken me?"

Matthew 27:46

Do not hide your face from me,
do not turn your servant away in anger;
you have been my helper.
Do not reject me or forsake me,
O God my Savior.

Psalm 27:9

My God, my God, why have you forsaken me?
Why are you so far from saving me,
so far from the words of my groaning?

Psalm 22:1

Jesus said to his disciples, "A time is coming, and has come, when you will be scattered, each to his own home. You will leave me all alone. Yet I am not alone, for my Father is with me."

John 16:32

You never have to hide your feelings of loneliness from God. Tell him how you feel. Even when you feel that no one else will listen to you, he will always be by your side, ready with a listening ear and a loving embrace.

Do not be far from me, O God,
for trouble is near
and there is no one to help.

Psalm 22:11

Turn, O LORD, and deliver me;
save me because of your unfailing love.

Psalm 6:4

This is the confidence we have in approaching God: that if we ask anything according to his will, he hears us. And if we know that he hears us—whatever we ask—we know that we have what we asked of him.

1 John 5:14–15

Jesus said, "Ask and it will be given to you; seek and you will find; knock and the door will be opened to you. For everyone who asks receives; he who seeks finds; and to him who knocks, the door will be opened."

Matthew 7:7–8

When we feel alone and abandoned, we can take comfort in God's promises to deliver us from our isolation and pain. God never forgets us.

"Can a mother forget the baby at her breast
  and have no compassion on the child she has borne?
Though she may forget,
  I will not forget you!
See, I have engraved you on the palms of my hands,"
declairs the LORD.

Isaiah 49:15–16

I sought the LORD, and he answered me;
  he delivered me from all my fears.

Psalm 34:4

For the sake of his great name, the LORD will not reject
his people, because the Lord was pleased to make you
his own.

1 Samuel 12:22

The LORD is good,
  a refuge in times of trouble.
He cares for those who trust in him.

Nahum 1:7

God is always with us—in our joy and in our pain, in the good times and in the bad times. His steadfast love and faithfulness are promises we can cling to, promises to bring us joy when we face loneliness.

I trust in your unfailing love;
  my heart rejoices in your salvation.
I will sing to the LORD,
  for he has been good to me.

Psalm 13:5–6

I have set the LORD always before me.
  Because he is at my right hand,
  I will not be shaken.
Therefore my heart is glad and my tongue rejoices;
  my body also will rest secure,
  because you will not abandon me.

Psalm 16:8–10

The LORD reached down from on high and took hold of me;
  he drew me out of deep waters. ...
He brought me out into a spacious place;
  he rescued me because he delighted in me.

Psalm 18:16, 19

Jesus said, "Now is your time of grief, but I will see you again and you will rejoice, and no one will take away your joy."

John 16:22

When loneliness overtakes us, we need to remember that we are not alone. God has promised to be with us. He will never forsake us. Lean on his promises and receive his peace.

Why are you downcast, O my soul?
  Why so disturbed within me?
Put your hope in God,
  for I will yet praise him,
  my Savior and my God.

Psalm 42:11

I will lie down and sleep in peace,
  for you alone, O LORD,
  make me dwell in safety.

Psalm 4:8

The Lord gives strength to his people;
  the Lord blesses his people with peace.

Psalm 29:11

I will listen to what God the LORD will say;
  he promises peace to his people, his saints.

Psalm 85:8

Imagine you're walking down the hall at school. You spot some of your friends hanging around in front of their lockers. You walk over to say hi. But when you get there, they all walk away. There you are, alone and rejected. It's the worst feeling in the world.

Earlier this year, some of my friends turned against me for no reason. I was so hurt and confused. I didn't know what to do. They wouldn't talk to me about what was going on, and I felt so helpless. But the experience taught me that even though my friends might turn against me, God never will. Even when I felt like I was all alone, God was there.

So when your friends let you down, remember that God is still there, ready to listen to you and help you get through hard times. He will be a friend to the end.

Jenna

I was in a musical based on the Psalms, and I sang a song called "My God, My God" based on the first few verses of Psalm 22. It was a pretty intense (and almost depressing) song with lots of questions and complaints to God. David was in bad shape when he wrote Psalm 22. And I can understand why Jesus quoted from this psalm when he was at his lowest point—dying on the cross.

But that's not the end of the psalm, or the end of the story. The ultimate message of the psalm is that God never leaves us—even when other people say he has, or when it seems like we're totally alone. He never abandoned David. He never abandoned Jesus. And he'll never abandon you or me.

Viannah

God Is *with* Us ...

In Our Sorrow

I realized that this was at the lowest and saddest times of my life.

Sorrow can cause us to doubt God's plan. Even the writer of Psalms wondered if God was still there and if he still cared: "Has his unfailing love vanished forever? Has his promise failed for all time? Has God forgotten to be merciful? Has he in anger withheld his compassion?" (Psalm 77:8–9). Though we may face trouble and difficulties, sadness and pain, God is still in control, and he is always with us.

My flesh and my heart may fail,
but God is the strength of my heart
and my portion forever.

Psalm 73:26

When I said, "My foot is slipping,"
your love, O LORD, supported me.

Psalm 94:18

The LORD upholds all those who fall
and lifts up all who are bowed down.

Psalm 145:14

The LORD is a refuge for the oppressed,
a stronghold in times of trouble.

Psalm 9:9

Life can sometimes leave us feeling completely crushed and lost. When terrible things happen, you may feel like you're the only one who has ever felt so bad. It may help to remember that as long as there have been people, bad things have happened to them.

Satan went out from the presence of the LORD *and afflicted Job with painful sores from the soles of his feet to the top of his head. ... His wife said to him, "Are you still holding on to your integrity? Curse God and die!"*

He replied, "You are talking like a foolish woman. Shall we accept good from God, and not trouble?" In all this, Job did not sin in what he said.

Job 2:7, 9–10

My guilt has overwhelmed me
like a burden too heavy to bear. ...
I am bowed down and brought very low;
all day long I go about mourning.
My back is filled with searing pain;
there is no health in my body.
I am feeble and utterly crushed;
I groan in anguish of heart.
All my longings lie open before you, O LORD*;*
my sighing is not hidden from you.

Psalm 38:4, 6–9

We are hard pressed on every side, but not crushed; perplexed, but not in despair; persecuted, but not aban-doned; struck down, but not destroyed.

2 Corinthians 4:8–9

What should help even more is to know that God has
been with all people who have suffered, comforting
and caring for them in dark times.

The LORD is close to the brokenhearted
    and saves those who are crushed in spirit.

Psalm 34:18

The LORD has heard my cry for mercy;
    the LORD accepts my prayer.

Psalm 6:9

The cords of death entangled me,
    the anguish of the grave came upon me;
    I was overcome by trouble and sorrow.
Then I called on the name of the LORD:
    "O LORD, save me!" ...
The LORD protects the simplehearted;
    when I was in great need, he saved me.
Be at rest once more, O my soul,
    for the LORD has been good to you.
For you, O LORD, have delivered my soul from death,
    my eyes from tears,
    my feet from stumbling,

Psalm 116:3–4, 6–8

My soul finds rest in God alone;
  my salvation comes from him.

Psalm 62:1

Jesus said, "Peace I leave with you; my peace I give you. I do not give to you as the world gives. Do not let your hearts be troubled and do not be afraid."

John 14:27

Praise be to the God and Father of our Lord Jesus Christ, the Father of compassion and the God of all comfort, who comforts us in all our troubles, so that we can comfort those in any trouble with the comfort we ourselves have received from God.

2 Corinthians 1:3–4

My comfort in my suffering is this:
  Your promise preserves my life.

Psalm 119:50

Jesus said, "My grace is sufficient for you, for my power is made perfect in weakness."

2 Corinthians 12:9

Even Jesus experienced deep sorrow while he was living on earth as one of us. In the Garden of Gethsemane, where he prayed the night before he died, the Bible says that Jesus was actually sweating blood because he was in such turmoil. Jesus did that for you, and when you experience deep sorrow, he'll be there to see you through it. He's been there and knows what it's like.

Probably the deepest sorrow we'll face in this life is losing people we love to death. But God reminds us that he is still in control. Death is not the master—God is!

Never again will they hunger;
  never again will they thirst.
The sun will not beat upon them,
  nor any scorching heat.
For the Lamb at the center of the throne
    will be their shepherd;
  he will lead them to springs of living water.
And God will wipe away every tear from their eyes

Revelation 7:16–17

Jesus said, "I am the resurrection and the life. He who believes in me will live, even though he dies; and whoever lives and believes in me will never die."

John 11:25–26

A student once asked, "A Christian friend of mine was killed by a drunk driver. Why does God allow bad things to happen to his people?" I can understand why he would ask that question. But when tragic things happen, we make a mistake if we blame them on God.

The Bible clearly says that God does not create evil (see Genesis 1:31 and 1 Timothy 4:4). Death came into the world when Adam and Eve sinned (see 1 Corinthians 15:21), and it's going to be with us until Jesus comes back. There are a ton of evil forces in the world that cause us pain—including death. But God is hard at work fighting these forces. And one day, he's going to destroy death (see 1 Corinthians 15:26). In the meantime, Jesus tells us that "in this world, you will have trouble. But take heart! I have overcome the world" (John 16:33).

I'm a college professor. Sometimes I ask my students, "What is the most evil thing that ever happened in human history? They always answer, "The crucifixion of Jesus!" Then I ask, "What is the most wonderful thing that ever happened in human history?" The same students say, "The crucifixion of Jesus!" This horrible event, which was the result of sin, was taken by God and transformed into something that has blessed people everywhere.

God doesn't make bad things happen, but he is at work in the middle of all things, overcoming evil with good and turning tragedy into blessings. So, instead of asking, "Why does God allow bad things to happen?" we should be asking, "What can God do through this tragedy? How can I work with God to turn this into something good?"

Tony Campolo

God Is *with* Us ...

Why Should We Worry?

This always bothered me ...

Worry and a kitchen blender have a lot in common. With the push of a button the contents of a blender are whirled and swirled until they become a frothy, churned mixture. In our lives, worry chews and gnaws and wears away at us until our lives become a churned jumble. But God doesn't want us to live "blender-ized" lives of worry.

Do not fret because of evil men
or be envious of those who do wrong;
for like the grass they will soon wither,
like green plants they will soon die away.
Trust in the LORD and do good.

Psalm 37:1–3

When anxiety was great within me,
your consolation brought joy to my soul, LORD.

Psalm 94:19

Jesus said, "Do not worry about your life, what you will eat; or about your body, what you will wear. Life is more than food, and the body more than clothes."

Luke 12:22–23

Jesus said, "Who of you by worrying can add a single hour to his life? And why do you worry about clothes? See how the lilies of the field grow. They do not labor or spin. Yet I tell you that not even Solomon in all his splendor was dressed like one of these. If that is how God clothes the grass of the field, which is here today and tomorrow is thrown into the fire, will he not much more clothe you?"

Matthew 6:27–3

Cast all your anxiety on God because he cares for you.

1 Peter 5:7

Do not be anxious about anything, but in everything, by prayer and petition, with thanksgiving, present your requests to God. And the peace of God, which transcends all understanding, will guard your hearts and your minds in Christ Jesus.

Philippians 4:6–7

I know that the Lₒʀᴅ saves his anointed;
  he answers him from his holy heaven
  with the saving power of his right hand.
Some trust in chariots and some in horses,
  but we trust in the name of the Lₒʀᴅ our God.
They are brought to their knees and fall,
  but we rise up and stand firm.

Psalm 20:6–8

The Lₒʀᴅ's unfailing love
  surrounds the man who trusts in him.

Psalm 32:10

Don't fret! Cheer up! Neither the sun, nor the Son, have gone out of business. He is with us. A new day will dawn, and the Lord will bring himself to the center of our problems.

Blessed is the man who trusts in the LORD,
    whose confidence is in him.
He will be like a tree planted by the water
    that sends out its roots by the stream.
It does not fear when heat comes;
    its leaves are always green.
It has no worries in a year of drought
    and never fails to bear fruit.

Jeremiah 17:7–8

Great peace have they who love your law,
    and nothing can make them stumble.

Psalm 119:165

Commit your way to the LORD;
    trust in him and he will do this:
He will make your righteousness shine like the dawn,
    the justice of your cause like the noonday sun.

Psalm 37:5–6

Worry has a lot to do with our perspective. If you're lost in the woods you can't see your way out because the trees are too close to you. But if you climb up to the top and look above it all, you can see that you're almost out of the woods! When you don't know which way to turn in life, remember that God can see your past, present, and future, and he'll show you where to go. Remember that things aren't always as they seem.

Elisha's servant saw only impending doom, but Elisha asked God to show him how things really were:

When the servant of the man of God [Elisha] got up and went out early the next morning, an army with horses and chariots had surrounded the city. "Oh, my lord, what shall we do?" the servant asked.

"Don't be afraid," the prophet answered. "Those who are with us are more than those who are with them."

And Elisha prayed, "O Lord, open his eyes so he may see." Then the Lord opened the servant's eyes, and he looked and saw the hills full of horses and chariots of fire all around Elisha.

2 Kings 6:15–17

It looked like certain death for three teens when they defied the king and refused to worship an idol. But when they were thrown into a blazing furnace, it became clear that they had nothing to worry about:

Nebuchadnezzar was furious with Shadrach, Meshach and Abednego. ... He ordered the furnace heated seven times hotter than usual and commanded some of the strongest soldiers in his army to tie up Shadrach, Meshach and Abednego and throw them into the blazing furnace. So these men, wearing their robes, trousers, turbans and other clothes, were bound and thrown into the blazing furnace. The king's command was so urgent and the furnace so hot that the flames of the fire killed the soldiers who took up Shadrach, Meshach and Abednego, and these three men, firmly tied, fell into the blazing furnace.

Then King Nebuchadnezzar leaped to his feet in amazement and asked his advisers, "Weren't there three men that we tied up and threw into the fire?"

They replied, "Certainly, O king."

He said, "Look! I see four men walking around in the fire, unbound and unharmed, and the fourth looks like a son of the gods."

Nebuchadnezzar then approached the opening of the blazing furnace and shouted, "Shadrach, Meshach and Abednego, servants of the Most High God, come out! Come here!"

So Shadrach, Meshach and Abednego came out of the fire, and the satraps, prefects, governors and royal advisers crowded around them. They saw that the fire had not harmed their bodies, nor was a hair of their heads singed; their robes were not scorched, and there was no smell of fire on them.

Daniel 3:19–27

Shadrach, Meshach, and Abednego's good pal, Daniel, also found himself in a seemingly hopeless situation. The king had ordered that no one should pray, unless they were praying to him. Daniel didn't miss a beat; he kept praying to God three times a day as usual. As a result he became the main dish in the lion's den. But he didn't need to worry ... God wasn't going to let him become cat food:

The king gave the order, and they brought Daniel and threw him into the lions' den. The king said to Daniel, "May your God, whom you serve continually, rescue you!"

A stone was brought and placed over the mouth of the den, and the king sealed it with his own signet ring and with the rings of his nobles, so that Daniel's situation might not be changed. ...

At the first light of dawn, the king got up and hurried to the lions' den. When he came near the den, he called to Daniel in an anguished voice, "Daniel, servant of the living God, has your God, whom you serve continually, been able to rescue you from the lions?"

Daniel answered, "O king, live forever! My God sent his angel, and he shut the mouths of the lions. They have not hurt me, because I was found innocent in his sight. Nor have I ever done any wrong before you, O king."

The king was overjoyed and gave orders to lift Daniel out of the den. And when Daniel was lifted from the den, no wound was found on him, because he had trusted in his God.

Daniel 6:16–17, 19–23

Surely this is our God;
   we trusted in him, and he saved us.
This is the LORD, we trusted in him.

Isaiah 25:9

God Is *with* Us ...

When We Need Direction

And I questioned the Lord about my dilemma.

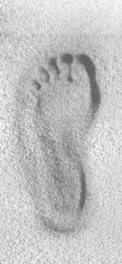

Remember inviting a friend to your house for the first time? Did you say, "Come on over. I'll see you when you get here" and leave it at that? Probably not, if you actually wanted her to still be your friend! You gave her specific directions so she would be sure to find her way to your door.

In the same way, God didn't create you and say, "You're on your own. Hope you figure out what to do with your life!" Instead, he actually wrote an entire book with specific instructions on how to live your life to the fullest. Are you feeling a little lost? Pick up the Bible —God's roadmap!

This is what the LORD says—
your Redeemer, the Holy One of Israel:
"I am the LORD your God,
who teaches you what is best for you,
who directs you in the way you should go."

Isaiah 48:17

A man's steps are directed by the LORD.

Proverbs 20:24

Let your eyes look straight ahead,
fix your gaze directly before you.
Make level paths for your feet
and take only ways that are firm.
Do not swerve to the right or the left;
keep your foot from evil.

Proverbs 4:25–27

Whether you turn to the right or to the left, your ears
will hear a voice behind you, saying, "This is the way;
walk in it."

Isaiah 30:21

Pay attention and listen to the sayings of the wise;
apply your heart to what I teach,
for it is pleasing when you keep them in your heart
and have all of them ready on your lips.

Proverbs 22:17–18

Your word is a lamp to my feet
and a light for my path, LORD.

Psalm 119:105

This is what the LORD says:
"Stand at the crossroads and look;
ask for the ancient paths,
ask where the good way is, and walk in it,
and you will find rest for your souls."

Jeremiah 6:16

When we need direction, we must trust that the Lord will take our faith, limited as it is, and make something of lasting value out of it. God has a plan for us. He cares about our dilemmas, hears our heartfelt cries and will answer us in ways that will astonish us and fill our hearts with songs of joy.

I know that you can do all things;
no plan of yours can be thwarted, O God.

Job 42:2

The plans of the Lord stand firm forever,
the purposes of his heart through all generations.

Psalm 33:11

"I know the plans I have for you," declares the Lord,
"plans to prosper you and not to harm you, plans to
give you hope and a future."

Jeremiah 29:11

Lord, you have assigned me my portion and my cup;
you have made my lot secure.
The boundary lines have fallen for me in pleasant
places;
surely I have a delightful inheritance.

Psalm 16:5–6

You can ask God for direction at any time. In fact, he wants you to seek the path he's set for you.

Jesus said, "I will show you what he is like who comes to me and hears my words and puts them into practice. He is like a man building a house, who dug down deep and laid the foundation on rock. When a flood came, the torrent struck that house but could not shake it, because it was well built."

Luke 6:47–48

Direct my footsteps according to your word, LORD.

Psalm 119:133

Direct me in the path of your commands,
  for there I find delight.

Psalm 119:35

May the Lord direct your hearts into God's love and Christ's perseverance.

2 Thessalonians 3:5

Show me your ways, O LORD,
  teach me your paths.

Psalm 25:4

We all get lost during our lives. Sometimes it just happens, but other times we get lost because we have strayed away from the path God has shown us. Even then, God is ready to find you and help you find your way again.

I have strayed like a lost sheep.
  Seek your servant, LORD,
    for I have not forgotten your commands.

Psalm 119:176

This is what the Sovereign LORD says: I myself will search for my sheep and look after them. As a shepherd looks after his scattered flock when he is with them, so will I look after my sheep. I will rescue them from all the places where they were scattered on a day of clouds and darkness. ... I myself will tend my sheep and have them lie down, declares the Sovereign LORD. I will search for the lost and bring back the strays. I will bind up the injured and strengthen the weak. ... I will shepherd the flock with justice.

Ezekiel 34:11–12, 15–16

Jesus said, "The Son of Man came to seek and to save what was lost."

Luke 19:10

I always prided myself on being able to find my way around any city or town throughout the world. My husband, Paul, would just give me a map and I would head out, perhaps with one of my children as co-pilot in the passenger seat, and be certain of finding my destination with ease. I found that this sense of direction gave me great freedom and independence.

Nevertheless, when we moved to British Columbia, I seemed to have great difficulty in finding my way anywhere and I had to put my faith in Paul and the map to take us across rivers and over winding mountain roads. Often, it all conflicted with my sense of where north, south, east and west lay. I could not understand it; navigating had previously been so easy.

Once, I was going to attend a children's meeting in a town I had not visited before. My young daughters were with me and, as the afternoon wore on, I realized I was hopelessly lost, although Paul had given me clear directions. Evening fell and the girls became alarmed; they just wanted Daddy to come and find us. It was long past the time that the children's meeting was due to start so I gave up and parked in a motel parking lot that overlooked a busy highway. Suddenly, there was a horrible sound of crunching metal and glass as ten cars piled into each other below us. Sirens began wailing and, in my anxiety, I imagined Paul out searching for us and getting caught in an accident somewhere.

Just at that moment, miraculously, he drew up along-side us. "Honey, are you all right? The church called me—I'll let them know I've found you." Perhaps it's no surprise I was never invited back there!

That day I learned an important lesson. No matter how much faith we have in our abilities, they can let us down. It is far better to put our trust in God who watches over us and protects us. A similar incident happened in Washington state which made me give up boasting about my sense of direction for good! Instead, as I set off on a journey, I often pray a prayer like this:

You can have faith to move mountains, but how many mountains need moving? All I need just now, Lord, is faith to know that you can move them if I need them moved.

Margaret Fishback Powers

God Is *with* Us ...

In Our Decisions

"Lord, you told me when I decided
to follow You ..."

E very day is full of decisions. They may be simple, like choosing that red sweater over the blue one, or they may be hard, like choosing the right college, career, or even a spouse. The next few years will be full of some major decisions. You can trust that God will show you the right choices if you ask his advice.

If any of you lacks wisdom, he should ask God, who gives generously to all without finding fault, and it will be given to him.

James 1:5

The Lord will instruct you and teach you in the way you should go;
he will counsel you and watch over you.

Psalm 32:8

My son, if you accept my words
and store up my commands within you,
turning your ear to wisdom
and applying your heart to understanding,
and if you call out for insight
and cry aloud for understanding,
and if you look for it as for silver
and search for it as for hidden treasure,
then you will understand the fear of the Lord
and find the knowledge of God.
For the Lord gives wisdom,
and from his mouth come knowledge and under standing.

Proverbs 2:1-6

May my cry come before you, O LORD;
   give me understanding according to your word.

Psalm 119:169

Pride only breeds quarrels,
   but wisdom is found in those who take advice.

Proverbs 13:10

Blessed is the man who finds wisdom,
   the man who gains understanding,
for she is more profitable than silver
   and yields better returns than gold.

Proverbs 3:13–14

My son, pay attention to my wisdom,
   listen well to my words of insight,
that you may maintain discretion
   and your lips may preserve knowledge.

Proverbs 5:1–2

To the man who pleases him, God gives wisdom, knowledge and happiness.

Ecclesiastes 2:26

Remember that God will sometimes use the people he's placed in your life to help you with decisions, people like pastors, teachers, even your parents. He also sent the greatest teacher of all, Jesus, whose example is always a reliable guide when making big choices.

Keep your father's commands
  and do not forsake your mother's teaching.
Bind them upon your heart forever;
  fasten them around your neck.
When you walk, they will guide you;
  when you sleep, they will watch over you;
  when you awake, they will speak to you.
For these commands are a lamp,
  this teaching is a light,
and the corrections of discipline
  are the way to life.

Proverbs 6:20–23

For lack of guidance a nation falls,
  but many advisers make victory sure.

Proverbs 11:14

So, what's the big deal about wisdom? Well, when you get true wisdom, the kind that comes straight from God, the Bible says that you'll be protected, successful and honored (just to name a few of the many benefits!).

The wisdom that comes from heaven is first of all pure; then peace-loving, considerate, submissive, full of mercy and good fruit, impartial and sincere.

James 3:17

Wisdom will enter your heart,
and knowledge will be pleasant to your soul.
Discretion will protect you,
and understanding will guard you.

Proverbs 2:10–11

Do not forsake wisdom, and she will protect you;
love her, and she will watch over you.
Wisdom is supreme; therefore get wisdom.
Though it cost all you have, get understanding.
Esteem her, and she will exalt you;
embrace her, and she will honor you.
She will set a garland of grace on your head
and present you with a crown of splendor.

Proverbs 4:6–9

Wisdom is more precious than rubies,
and nothing you desire can compare with her.

Proverbs 8:11

He who gets wisdom loves his own soul;
  he who cherishes understanding prospers.

Proverbs 19:8

A man's wisdom gives him patience;
  it is to his glory to overlook an offense.

Proverbs 19:11

By wisdom a house is built,
  and through understanding it is established;
through knowledge its rooms are filled
  with rare and beautiful treasures.

Proverbs 24:3–4

Know also that wisdom is sweet to your soul;
  if you find it, there is a future hope for you,
  and your hope will not be cut off.

Proverbs 24:14

Wisdom, like an inheritance, is a good thing
  and benefits those who see the sun.
Wisdom is a shelter
  as money is a shelter,
but the advantage of knowledge is this:
  that wisdom preserves the life of its possessor.

Ecclesiastes 7:11–12

OK, I know it's probably going to be a long time before you're a parent, but just imagine it for a moment: You've got a son named Chad. You've hidden a treasure chest full of Chad's favorite stuff in the backyard, and you tell him to go find it. He's excited, but he's got a ton of questions like, "How will I know where to find it?" and "Where do I start?" You hand him a map and tell him you've marked out the path to the treasure.

Chad grabs the map and heads toward the swings. You gently guide him toward an old oak tree. Then Chad notices the sandbox and starts heading for it; you lovingly turn him toward the old oak tree again. Then Chad stops and tosses a Frisbee to his dog, and then he heads for the garden. Again, you gently turn him toward the old oak tree. As a loving parent, you're constantly guiding Chad toward the treasure, because you want to make sure he finds it.

It works the same way spiritually. God, your heavenly Father, has an incredible plan for your life, and he's given you a wonderful map—the Bible, the guide for your path. But you have to read it, learn it and apply it to your life. If you do this and still end up taking the wrong turn, God will gently turn you around and guide you in the right direction. You see, God wants you to fulfill his plan for your life even more than you can imagine.

It's God's responsibility to make sure we "get" his plan; it's our responsibility to communicate with him often. But communicating with God means more than just talking to him. We've got to listen too. Sometimes we're so busy talking to God that we forget to listen for his voice.

God uses other ways to show us his will. He also works through our thoughts, our interests, our spiritual leaders (pastor, youth minister, parents, church school teacher) and our gifts. God has given you specific gifts and abilities to use for his glory. So use 'em! If you're a real "people-person," for example, God's will for you probably includes working with people.

When seeking God's will for your life, it's important to remember that "God's will" doesn't simply mean what your career will be, whom you'll marry and where you'll live. Those things are only parts of his will. His plan for you includes the things going on in your life right now, at this very moment. So instead of asking God what he wants you to do in five years from now, ask him, "Lord, help me to be all you want me to be. What is your will for me today?"

Susie Shellenberger

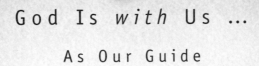

God Is *with* Us ...

As Our Guide

"... You would walk and talk with me
all the way."

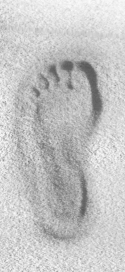

When you were a little kid, knowing the difference between right and wrong was pretty simple. Wrong was hitting your sister or sneaking cookies before dinner. Right was obeying your parents and eating all your vegetables.

Now you're not so little anymore and all of a sudden right and wrong don't seem so simple. Is it okay to be alone with my boyfriend or girlfriend? Should I go to that party where there will be drinking, even though I know I won't drink? I'm learning some things in science class that I'm not sure go along with the Bible. Should I speak up about them or stay silent out of respect for my teacher? Wow ... when did life get so complicated? When you're faced with these kinds of problems, remember that God is there to guide you.

The LORD will guide you always;
he will satisfy your needs in a sun-scorched land
and will strengthen your frame.
You will be like a well-watered garden,
like a spring whose waters never fail.

Isaiah 58:11

God guides me in paths of righteousness
for his name's sake.

Psalm 23:3

God is our God for ever and ever;
he will be our guide even to the end.

Psalm 48:14

*You guide me with your counsel, L*ORD*,*
   and afterward you will take me into glory.

Psalm 73:24

"I will lead the blind by ways they have not known,
   along unfamiliar paths I will guide them;
I will turn the darkness into light before them
   and make the rough places smooth.
These are the things I will do;
   *I will not forsake them," says the L*ORD*.*

Isaiah 42:16

In your unfailing love you will lead
   *the people you have redeemed, O L*ORD*.*
In your strength you will guide them
   to your holy dwelling.

Exodus 15:13

God guides the humble in what is right
   and teaches them his way.

Psalm 25:9

How do you get God's guidance? All you have to do is ask.

Guide me in your truth and teach me,
for you are God my Savior,
and my hope is in you all day long.

Psalm 25:5

Since you are my rock and my fortress, LORD,
for the sake of your name lead and guide me.

Psalm 31:3

Send forth your light and your truth, O God,
let them guide me;
let them bring me to your holy mountain,
to the place where you dwell.

Psalm 43:3

Lead me, O LORD, in your righteousness ...
make straight your way before me.

Psalm 5:8

When you ask for God's guidance, he'll give it to you in many ways. First of all, he'll give you his Spirit. He'll also speak to you through the Bible and through other people in your life, like parents and godly friends. If you take time to listen, you'll find that God's guidance is all around you!

Jesus said, "When he, the Spirit of truth, comes, he will guide you into all truth. He will not speak on his own; he will speak only what he hears, and he will tell you what is yet to come."

John 16:13

The integrity of the upright guides them.

Proverbs 11:3

Let the wise listen and add to their learning,
and let the discerning get guidance.

Proverbs 1:5

The grace of God that brings salvation has appeared to all men. It teaches us to say "No" to ungodliness and worldly passions, and to live self-controlled, upright and godly lives in this present age, while we wait for the blessed hope—the glorious appearing of our great God and Savior, Jesus Christ.

Titus 2:11–13

As you get older, you're going to find that there are a lot of "gray areas" in life—issues that are not clearly black or white, right or wrong.

There are two extremes to avoid when making decisions on gray areas. The first one is license—that's the party-on attitude that says, "Hey, if it's not illegal, it's fine." The other extreme is just as dangerous. It's called legalism, which is thinking that you have to obey a huge list of do's and don'ts in order to be close to God.

Between these two extremes is real liberty, the ability to enjoy what's good in life while avoiding what's bad. Here are four questions that can help you when you encounter a gray area:

Will it please God? Avoid anything that God will eventually judge and destroy.

Will it help me? Think about whether the activity is beneficial for your health and spiritual growth.

Could it enslave me? If the activity is tempting, addicting or really time-consuming, watch out.

Will it hurt someone else? How would it feel to be in their shoes?

Put your questionable activities to these tests, and you're likely to find your way through life's gray areas.

The Teen Devotional Bible

God Is *with* Us ...

In Our Difficulties

"But I'm aware that during the most troublesome times of my life there is only one set of footprints."

L *ife is hard.* There's just no getting around this fact. Even though we are following God, things still get really difficult. People we love get sick and die. Sometimes our dreams end up in disappointment. And with wars and famines and sickness, the world sometimes seems to be falling apart.

You're not alone in feeling troubled by all this turmoil. The Bible records many times when people looked around at their world and felt overwhelmed and alone.

A prophet named Elijah stood up for God against an evil king. The king's equally evil wife was so enraged by Elijah that she promised to have him killed. Elijah ran for his life and ended up so afraid and overwhelmed that he was ready to give up. But God was still there.

When Elijah came to Beersheba in Judah, he left his servant there, while he himself went a day's journey into the desert. He came to a broom tree, sat down under it and prayed that he might die. "I have had enough, Lord," he said. "Take my life; I am no better than my ancestors." Then he lay down under the tree and fell asleep.

All at once an angel touched him and said, "Get up and eat." He looked around, and there by his head was a cake of bread baked over hot coals, and a jar of water. He ate and drank and then lay down again.

The angel of the Lord came back a second time and touched him and said, "Get up and eat, for the journey is too much for you." So he got up and ate and drank. Strengthened by that food, he traveled forty days and forty nights until he reached Horeb, the mountain of God.

1 Kings 19:3–8

Sometimes God asks us to do something difficult in order to serve him. Jonah was asked to do something really hard; he was called to bring the good news of God's forgiveness to a city called Nineveh. It would be like God telling you to go talk about God's love to a bunch of terrorists who wanted nothing more than to kill you. So Jonah decided to run the other way and ignore God's call. Then things got a lot more difficult than he'd bargained for.

The word of the LORD came to Jonah son of Amittai: "Go to the great city of Nineveh and preach against it, because its wickedness has come up before me."

But Jonah ran away from the LORD and headed for Tarshish. He went down to Joppa, where he found a ship bound for that port. After paying the fare, he went aboard and sailed for Tarshish to flee from the LORD.

Then the LORD sent a great wind on the sea, and such a violent storm arose that the ship threatened to break up. All the sailors were afraid and each cried out to his own god. ...

Jonah had gone below deck, where he lay down and fell into a deep sleep. The captain went to him and said, "How can you sleep? Get up and call on your god! Maybe he will take notice of us, and we will not perish." ...

The sea was getting rougher and rougher. So they asked him, "What should we do to you to make the sea calm down for us?"

"Pick me up and throw me into the sea," he replied, "and it will become calm. I know that it is my fault that this great storm has come upon you."

Instead, the men did their best to row back to land. But they could not, for the sea grew even wilder than before. Then they cried to the LORD, "O LORD, please do not let us die for taking this man's life. Do not hold us accountable for killing an innocent man, for you, O LORD, have done as you pleased." Then they took Jonah and threw him overboard, and the raging sea grew calm.

Jonah 1:1–6, 11–15

But that's not the end of Jonah's story. God was still there, even though Jonah ran from him. God didn't let Jonah drown. He provided an interesting place for Jonah to "chill" and think about what he'd done. In this place, Jonah realized what a mess he'd made of things, and God brought him to where he should have gone in the first place:

The Lord provided a great fish to swallow Jonah, and Jonah was inside the fish three days and three nights.

From inside the fish Jonah prayed to the LORD his God. He said:
"In my distress I called to the LORD,
  and he answered me.
From the depths of the grave I called for help,
  and you listened to my cry.
You hurled me into the deep,
  into the very heart of the seas,
  and the currents swirled about me;
all your waves and breakers
  swept over me.

I said, 'I have been banished
   from your sight;
   yet I will look again
   toward your holy temple.'
The engulfing waters threatened me,
   the deep surrounded me;
   seaweed was wrapped around my head.
To the roots of the mountains I sank down;
   the earth beneath barred me in forever.
   But you brought my life up from the pit,
   O LORD my God.
"When my life was ebbing away,
   I remembered you, LORD,
and my prayer rose to you,
   to your holy temple.
"Those who cling to worthless idols
   forfeit the grace that could be theirs.
But I, with a song of thanksgiving,
   will sacrifice to you.
What I have vowed I will make good.
   Salvation comes from the LORD."
And the LORD commanded the fish, and it vomited Jonah
onto dry land.

Jonah 1:17 — 2:10

God has been in the business of helping people through difficulties for a long, long time. You can count on the fact that he'll be there to help you, too, when you call on him.

For Christ's sake, I delight in weaknesses, in insults, in hardships, in persecutions, in difficulties. For when I am weak, then I am strong.

2 Corinthians 12:10

Do not be afraid. Stand firm and you will see the deliverance the LORD will bring you today. ... The LORD will fight for you; you need only to be still.

Exodus 14:13–14

Ah, Sovereign LORD, you have made the heavens and the earth by your great power and outstretched arm. Nothing is too hard for you.

Jeremiah 32:17

The LORD is my rock, my fortress and my deliverer;
my God is my rock, in whom I take refuge,
my shield and the horn of my salvation.
He is my stronghold, my refuge and my savior.

2 Samuel 22:2–3

I believe one reason God allows us to experience hard things in our lives is so we can become the warriors God wants us to become. God wants people of integrity who are tough, tested, confident, strong and courageous. He wants battle-worn soldiers who know what it's like to be in the trenches and aren't afraid of a challenge. Allowing battles and difficulties to come into our lives ensures a training ground to grow the kind of troops God is looking for to change the world.

Another reason God allows tough times is so we learn to look beyond the here and now and to him, heaven and our spiritual future. It is very easy to get sucked into the world, but when God allows something to rock our world, it is often a wake-up call to pay attention to what is the most important. Not only that, but he also uses struggles in our lives to open the eyes of people around us. I don't know how many times people have said to me that through my struggles they have come to know God or gained a new perspective on what difficulty, challenge and adversity are all about.

One thing I have learned when I am going through a particularly tough time is to take a look around me. Ninety-nine percent of the time I can find someone who is in a much worse situation than I am, and all of a sudden I have a lot to be thankful for and my situation doesn't seen so bad.

I have also learned that God doesn't put me through hard times for his enjoyment. The hard stuff in life is for something important, so I better pay attention and get the most I possibly can out the experience. Otherwise, I am wasting time and wasting an opportunity to be a part of something great.

Although it might be hard to see the good in a terrible situation, we can trust that God will use it someday, somehow for something incredible, and all the bad that happened in that situation will somehow be turned toward his glory and the good of those who trust him.

Michelle Akers, member of the
gold medal-winning US Olympic soccer team

God Is *with* Us ...

In Our Confusion

> *"I just don't understand why, when I needed You most, You leave me."*

Being a teen can be a confusing time. There are lots of big decisions looming in your future. You're trying to figure out who you are and what God wants you to be. On top of all this, friends move away, people get cancer, parents divorce and there seems to be bad news happening all over the world.

God seems far away when so much is happening that we don't understand. Even the Bible writers asked "Why?" sometimes.

Has God's unfailing love vanished forever?
  Has his promise failed for all time?
Has God forgotten to be merciful?
  Has he in anger withheld his compassion?

Psalm 77:8–9

O Lord, how many are my foes!
  How many rise up against me!
Many are saying of me,
  "God will not deliver him."

Psalm 3:1–2

Be merciful to me, Lord, for I am faint;
  O Lord, heal me, for my bones are in agony.
My soul is in anguish.
  How long, O Lord, how long?

Psalm 6:2–3

If I have sinned, what have I done to you,
  O watcher of men?
Why have you made me your target?
  Have I become a burden to you?
Why do you not pardon my offenses
  and forgive my sins?
For I will soon lie down in the dust;
  you will search for me, but I will be no more.

Job 7:20–21

Even God's own Son, Jesus, called out to his Father with questions as he faced his coming death.

They went to a place called Gethsemane, and Jesus said to his disciples, "Sit here while I pray." He took Peter, James and John along with him, and he began to be deeply distressed and troubled. "My soul is overwhelmed with sorrow to the point of death," he said to them. "Stay here and keep watch."

Going a little farther, he fell to the ground and prayed that if possible the hour might pass from him. "Abba, Father," he said, "everything is possible for you. Take this cup from me. Yet not what I will, but what you will."

Mark 14:32–36

At the ninth hour Jesus cried out in a loud voice, "Eloi, Eloi, lama sabachthani?"—which means, "My God, my God, why have you forsaken me?"

Mark 15:34

Sometimes when we ask "Why?" God shows us the answer clearly. Other times, he simply lets us know that he stills loves us, but it is not for us to know all his reasons. It's hard to not get the answers we want, but God knows best, and sometimes we have to just rest in that.

"Be still, and know that I am God."

Psalm 46:10

There is a time for everything,
   and a season for every activity under heaven.

Ecclesiastes 3:1

When times are good, be happy;
   but when times are bad, consider:
God has made the one
   as well as the other.

Ecclesiastes 7:14

"My thoughts are not your thoughts,
   neither are your ways my ways," declares the LORD.
"As the heavens are higher than the earth,
   so are my ways higher than your ways
   and my thoughts than your thoughts."

Isaiah 55:8–9

When faced with bewildering circumstances we are tempted to ask "Why?" But a better question to ask is "What? ... What do you have in mind now, Lord?"

"Call to me and I will answer you and tell you great and unsearchable things you do not know," says the Lord.

Jeremiah 33:3

"I make known the end from the beginning,
from ancient times, what is still to come.
I say: My purpose will stand,
and I will do all that I please...
What I have said, that will I bring about;
what I have planned, that will I do," says the Lord.

Isaiah 46:10–11

This is my prayer: that your love may abound more and more in knowledge and depth of insight, so that you may be able to discern what is best and may be pure and blameless until the day of Christ, filled with the fruit of righteousness that comes through Jesus Christ— to the glory and praise of God.

Philippians 1:9–11

Though it may sometimes seem that things are out of control, we can take comfort in God's enduring promises and constant presence.

You, O LORD, are a compassionate and gracious God,
  slow to anger, abounding in love and faithfulness.

Psalm 86:15

Who is a God like you,
  who pardons sin and forgives the transgression
  of the remnant of his inheritance?
You do not stay angry forever
  but delight to show mercy.
You will again have compassion on us.

Micah 7:18–19

This I call to mind
  and therefore I have hope:
Because of the Lord's great love we are not consumed,
  for his compassions never fail.
They are new every morning;
  great is your faithfulness.

Lamentations 3:21–23

We've all experienced doubts about God. We may wonder, *Is God real? Is he fair? Does he care?*

Having a case of the doubts doesn't mean you're a bad person. It just means you need something to boost your belief system. After all, being a Christian is all about believing what others don't.

Most of the great "giants" of the faith had doubts at least some of the time. Job was the greatest man of his day (Job 1:3), yet he doubted God's fairness. John the Baptist was the greatest of the prophets (Matthew 11:11), yet he doubted that Jesus was the Messiah (Matthew 11:2). David was a man after God's own heart (1 Samuel 13:14), yet he expressed strong doubts about God's presence in many of his psalms (see Psalm 13, for example).

When you doubt, take heart. You're in good company. When Thomas doubted the resurrection, Jesus gave him proof (John 20:27). When a doubting man asked for a miracle, Jesus helped him (Mark 9:17–27). In fact, the Bible commands us to be merciful to those who doubt (Jude 22).

So if you get the doubts, know that healing is available. Identify which strain of the doubting disease you have, then take the appropriate medicine. Here are three common symptoms:

1. "God's not fair!"

Sometimes terrible tragedies cause us to doubt God's goodness or fairness. And, like Job, we complain about it. Loudly. That's good; God can handle that. In fact, he would rather we express our doubts than ignore them. The best medicine in this case is prayer and patience. Just tell God how you feel and wait for him to remind you of his kindness and love.

2. "It's not true!"

Do you ever wonder, Is God real? Is the Bible true? Is Jesus the only way? These doubts deal with factual matters, and even people like John the Baptist faced them. In Matthew 11:4-5 he doubted whether Jesus was really the Messiah, so Jesus gave him a dose of proof positive. He told John's friends to "Go back and report to John what you hear and see: The blind receive sight, the lame walk, those who have leprosy are cured, the deaf hear, the dead are raised, and the good news is preached to the poor." That's what we need sometimes too. If you doubt the basic truth of God or his Word, talk to your pastor or your parents. There are very good reasons why we believe.

3. "I'm not sure!"

Sometimes we doubt our own faith. We wonder if we really belong to God or if we're really going to heaven. In this case, pop some promise pills. John 6:37 says Jesus will never drive away those who come to him. John 10:28 says no one can snatch God's people from his hand. Romans 8:38-39 says nothing can separate us from God's love. Thankfully, your salvation does not rest on the strength of your faith but on the power of God's promises. Take that medicine, and you'll start feeling much better!

Teen Devotional Bible

God Is *with* Us ...

As Our Loving Father

He whispered, "My precious child ..."

Lots of us have great dads—dads who play with us, pray with us, and love us. Some of us have not so great dads, and some don't have dads at all. No matter if you have a great dad or no dad, God is there to be your loving father—one who will never let you down.

How great is the love the Father has lavished on us, that we should be called children of God! And that is what we are! ... Dear friends, now we are children of God, and what we will be has not yet been made known. But we know that when he appears, we shall be like him, for we shall see him as he is.

1 John 3:1-2

"I will be a Father to you,
  and you will be my sons and daughters,
  says the Lord Almighty."

2 Corinthians 6:18

You did not receive a spirit that makes you a slave again to fear, but you received the Spirit of sonship. And by him we cry, "Abba, Father." The Spirit himself testifies with our spirit that we are God's children. Now if we are children, then we are heirs—heirs of God and co-heirs with Christ, if indeed we share in his sufferings in order that we may also share in his glory.

Romans 8:15-17

O Lord, you are our Father.
  We are the clay, you are the potter;
  we are all the work of your hand.

Isaiah 64:8

Praise be to the God and Father of our Lord Jesus Christ,
who has blessed us in the heavenly realms with every
spiritual blessing in Christ. For he chose us in him before
the creation of the world to be holy and blameless in
his sight. In love he predestined us to be adopted as
his sons through Jesus Christ, in accordance with his
pleasure and will—to the praise of his glorious grace,
which he has freely given us in the One he loves.

Ephesians 1:3–6

You are my Father,
  my God, the Rock my Savior.

Psalm 89:26

Jesus said, "The Father himself loves you because you
have loved me and have believed that I came from God."

John 16:27

To all who received Christ, to those who believed in his name, he gave the right to become children of God—children born not of natural descent, nor of human decision or a husband's will, but born of God.

John 1:12–13

As a father has compassion on his children,
  *so the L**ORD** has compassion on those who fear him.*

Psalm 103:13

There is one body and one Spirit—just as you were called to one hope when you were called—one Lord, one faith, one baptism; one God and Father of all, who is over all and through all and in all.

Ephesians 4:4–6

A father to the fatherless ...
  is God in his holy dwelling.
God sets the lonely in families.

Psalm 68:5–6

Jesus said, "Which of you fathers, if your son asks for a fish, will give him a snake instead? Or if he asks for an egg, will give him a scorpion? If you then ... know how to give good gifts to your children, how much more will your Father in heaven give the Holy Spirit to those who ask him!"

Luke 11:11–13

Like a good earthly father, God the Father helps us learn how to live our lives for him through discipline and guidance. Being disciplined is rarely fun (remember the last time you were grounded?), but God promises that later you'll reap some great rewards if you learn from his lessons.

"Do not make light of the Lord's discipline,
*   and do not lose heart when he rebukes you,*
because the Lord disciplines those he loves,
*   and he punishes everyone he accepts as a son."*

Endure hardship as discipline; God is treating you as sons. For what son is not disciplined by his father? ... Moreover, we have all had human fathers who disciplined us and we respected them for it. How much more should we submit to the Father of our spirits and live! Our fathers disciplined us for a little while as they thought best; but God disciplines us for our good, that we may share in his holiness. No discipline seems pleasant at the time, but painful. Later on, however, it produces a harvest of righteousness and peace for those who have been trained by it.

Hebrews 12:5–7, 9–11

The Lord disciplines those he loves,
*   as a father the son he delights in.*

Proverbs 3:12

The God of the universe calls us his children! Realizing that amazing fact should make us want to obey our perfect Father and love him with all our hearts.

We know that anyone born of God does not continue to sin; the one who was born of God keeps him safe, and the evil one cannot harm him.

1 John 5:18

Do everything without complaining or arguing, so that you may become blameless and pure, children of God without fault in a crooked and depraved generation, in which you shine like stars in the universe.

Philippians 2:14–15

For you were once darkness, but now you are light in the Lord. Live as children of light (for the fruit of the light consists in all goodness, righteousness and truth) and find out what pleases the Lord.

Ephesians 5:8–10

Be imitators of God, therefore, as dearly loved children and live a life of love, just as Christ loved us and gave himself up for us as a fragrant offering and sacrifice to God.

Ephesians 5:1–2

"Come over here. Right now."

These words would sound scary coming from that big bully at school, but keep reading.

"Come over here. Right now. Because I love you. All I want to do is help you. I will take care of you."

Sounds different now, doesn't it? That's because it's really God saying those words to you, not some tough guy at school. God wants you to come near to him, not because he's mean but because he loves you. And he wants you to get to know him right now.

But how do you get close to him? It's pretty easy, really. It's through God's grace. Try thinking of grace like God's hand reaching out to you to pull you close to him. That doesn't mean that God's big arm is a trac-tor-beam that's going to pull you into the sky and fly you to heaven right this second. What it does mean is that he's asking you to become like a little kid, crawl-ing up into his big, soft lap, giving every part of your life to him.

Sometimes you might not want to give God every part of your life, but when you do give him all of yourself life gets really good! He's so smart and good that he will take better care of you than anyone else—including you.

The closer you get to God, the more you experience the cool stuff that comes with having him as your perfect Father and best friend. Paul writes about some of this cool stuff in Galatians 5:22–23:

Joy. Even if your bike gets stolen, you can still be grateful for the other stuff that you have (Philippians 4:4).

Peace. When your best friend is getting ready to move to another state, you won't freak out (Philippians 4:6–7).

Gentleness. If everyone else in your class is making fun of the girl with the big teeth who sits in front of you, you make an extra effort to be kind to her (Philippians 4:5).

Self-control. When you are tempted to check out the websites and chat rooms you know you shouldn't, you shut down your computer and phone a friend instead (2 Timothy 1:7).

Can you feel God's hand reaching out to you like a loving daddy? Ask him to draw you close. Today.

Teen Devotional Bible

God Is *with* Us ...

Always!

> *"I love you and will never leave you never, ever, during your trials and testings."*

Nothing in this world is permanent. You are changing every day, and so is everyone else. Friendships that you thought would last a lifetime fade away. People you thought would always be there die. Nothing lasts forever. Nothing, that is, except God. When everything else seems to crumble around you, God is your solid place to stand. He never changes and he never goes away. His promises will never fail.

You are always righteous, O Lord.

Jeremiah 12:1

The Lord is good and his love endures forever;
   his faithfulness continues through all generations.

Psalm 100:5

He is the Lord our God;
   his judgments are in all the earth.
He remembers his covenant forever,
   the word he commanded, for a thousand generations.

1 Chronicles 16:14–15

Give thanks to the Lord, for he is good;
   his love endures forever.

1 Chronicles 16:34

From everlasting to everlasting
the Lord's love is with those who fear him,
and his righteousness with their children's children.

Psalm 103:17

Surely goodness and love will follow me
all the days of my life,
and I will dwell in the house of the Lord
forever.

Psalm 23:6

The Lord loves the just
and will not forsake his faithful ones.
They will be protected forever ...
the righteous will inherit the land
and dwell in it forever.

Psalm 37:28–29

In my integrity you uphold me
and set me in your presence forever.
Praise be to the Lord, the God of Israel,
from everlasting to everlasting.
Amen and Amen.

Psalm 41:12–13

I will sing of the LORD's great love forever;
*   with my mouth I will make your faithfulness known*
through all generations.
I will declare that your love stands firm forever,
*   that you established your faithfulness in heaven itself.*

Psalm 89:1–2

Great are the works of the LORD;
*   they are pondered by all who delight in them.*
Glorious and majestic are his deeds,
*   and his righteousness endures forever.*
He has caused his wonders to be remembered;
*   the LORD is gracious and compassionate.*
He provides food for those who fear him;
*   he remembers his covenant forever.*
He has shown his people the power of his works,
*   giving them the lands of other nations.*
The works of his hands are faithful and just;
*   all his precepts are trustworthy.*
They are steadfast for ever and ever,
*   done in faithfulness and uprightness.*
He provided redemption for his people;
*   he ordained his covenant forever—*
*   holy and awesome is his name.*

Psalm 111:2–9

Great is God's love toward us,
  and the faithfulness of the LORD endures forever.

Psalm 117:2

The word of the Lord stands forever.

1 Peter 1:25

"I the LORD do not change."

Malachi 3:6

Jesus Christ is the same yesterday and today and forever.

Hebrews 13:8

Your word, O LORD, is eternal;
  it stands firm in the heavens.

Psalm 119:89

God has made everything beautiful in its time. He has also set eternity in the hearts of men; yet they cannot fathom what God has done from beginning to end.

Ecclesiastes 3:11

Trust in the LORD forever,
  for the LORD, the LORD, is the Rock eternal.

Isaiah 26:4

God loves us so much that he wants to share forever with us. He wants us to know eternal joy and peace with him!

We believe that Jesus died and rose again and so we believe that God will bring with Jesus those who have fallen asleep in him. According to the Lord's own word, we tell you that we who are still alive, who are left till the coming of the Lord, will certainly not precede those who have fallen asleep. For the Lord himself will come down from heaven, with a loud command, with the voice of the archangel and with the trumpet call of God, and the dead in Christ will rise first. After that, we who are still alive and are left will be caught up together with them in the clouds to meet the Lord in the air. And so we will be with the Lord forever.

1 Thessalonians 4:14–17

God raised us up with Christ and seated us with him in the heavenly realms in Christ Jesus, in order that in the coming ages he might show the incomparable riches of his grace, expressed in his kindness to us in Christ Jesus.

Ephesians 2:6–7

Jesus said, "God so loved the world that he gave his one and only Son, that whoever believes in him shall not perish but have eternal life."

John 3:16

Jesus said, "My Father's will is that everyone who looks to the Son and believes in him shall have eternal life, and I will raise him up at the last day."

John 6:40

Our light and momentary troubles are achieving for us an eternal glory that far outweighs them all. So we fix our eyes not on what is seen, but on what is unseen. For what is seen is temporary, but what is unseen is eternal.

Now we know that if the earthly tent we live in is destroyed, we have a building from God, an eternal house in heaven, not built by human hands.

2 Corinthians 5:1

God has given us eternal life, and this life is in his Son.

1 John 5:11

Jesus said, "In my Father's house are many rooms; if it were not so, I would have told you. I am going there to prepare a place for you. And if I go and prepare a place for you, I will come back and take you to be with me that you also may be where I am."

John 14:2–3

I heard a loud voice from the throne saying, "Now the dwelling of God is with men, and he will live with them. They will be his people, and God himself will be with them and be their God. He will wipe every tear from their eyes. There will be no more death or mourning or crying or pain, for the old order of things has passed away."

Revelation 21:3–4

If you ever think that maybe God's forgotten the world, read Isaiah 9:2–7. Way back when the Old Testament was written, this prophet named Isaiah knew that people felt pretty hopeless. They had been through a lot of pain and suffering and thought it would never end.

But Isaiah promised them things would get better. He told the people about a baby who would save the world from sin. He told them that this baby would be the Son of God and that he would bring everlasting peace. It might have been hard for the people to believe Isaiah. Maybe they thought he was crazy for talking that way.

But we know Isaiah wasn't crazy. God did send his Son to live and die for us. When we accept Jesus as our Savior, we will have everlasting peace. We are God's children, and he will never leave us. That's a pretty amazing promise, and it's a promise we can count on.

Thank God today for keeping his promises and giving us hope for an incredible life with him!

Laura

God Is *with* Us ...

As Our Strong Provider

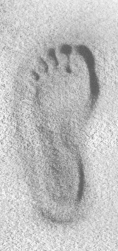

"When you saw only one set of footprints, it was then that I carried you."

No matter what troubles we face, God is bigger and stronger than them all. He is willing and able to give us everything we need and to help us overcome life's problems.

Jesus said, "With God all things are possible."

Matthew 19:26

The foolishness of God is wiser than man's wisdom, and the weakness of God is stronger than man's strength.

1 Corinthians 1:25

It is God who arms me with strength
and makes my way perfect.
He makes my feet like the feet of a deer;
he enables me to stand on the heights.

2 Samuel 22:33–34

One thing God has spoken,
two things have I heard:
that you, O God, are strong,
and that you, O LORD, are loving.

Psalm 62:11–12

God does as he pleases
  with the powers of heaven
  and the peoples of the earth.
No one can hold back his hand
  or say to him: "What have you done?"

Daniel 4:35

Wealth and honor come from you, LORD;
  you are the ruler of all things.
In your hands are strength and power
  to exalt and give strength to all.
Now, our God, we give you thanks,
  and praise your glorious name.

1 Chronicles 29:12–13

LORD, you established peace for us;
  all that we have accomplished you have done for us.

Isaiah 26:12

Blessed are those whose strength is in you, LORD. ...
They go from strength to strength,
  till each appears before God in Zion.

Psalm 84:5, 7

*I am honored in the eyes of the L*ORD
  and my God has been my strength.

Isaiah 49:5

*The L*ORD *is my strength and my song;*
  he has become my salvation.
He is my God, and I will praise him,
  my father's God, and I will exalt him.

Exodus 15:2

The God of all grace, who called you to his eternal glory
in Christ, after you have suffered a little while, will him-
self restore you and make you strong, firm and steadfast.

1 Peter 5:10

God is faithful; he will not let you be tempted beyond
what you can bear. But when you are tempted, he will
also provide a way out so that you can stand up under it.

1 Corinthians 10:13

In God, whose word I praise,
  in God I trust; I will not be afraid.
  What can mortal man do to me?

Psalm 56:4

When all your strength is gone and you feel like you can't go on anymore, know that God will lift you up in his strong arms and carry you all the way.

*The L*ORD *tends his flock like a shepherd:*
   He gathers the lambs in his arms
and carries them close to his heart;
   he gently leads those that have young.

Isaiah 40:11

*The L*ORD *is the strength of his people,*
   a fortress of salvation for his anointed one.
Save your people and bless your inheritance;
   be their shepherd and carry them forever.

Psalm 28:8–9

"I have made you and I will carry you;
   I will sustain you and I will rescue you,"
      *says the L*ORD.

Isaiah 46:4

"As a mother comforts her child,
   *so will I comfort you," says the L*ORD.

Isaiah 66:13

I will tell of the kindnesses of the LORD,
*   the deeds for which he is to be praised,*
*   according to all the Lord has done for us—*
yes, the many good things he has done
*   for the house of Israel,*
*   according to his compassion and many kindnesses. ...*
In all their distress he too was distressed,
*   and the angel of his presence saved them.*
In his love and mercy he redeemed them;
*   he lifted them up and carried them*
*   all the days of old.*

Isaiah 63:7, 9

God will command his angels concerning you
*   to guard you in all your ways;*
they will lift you up in their hands,
*   so that you will not strike your foot against a stone.*

Psalm 91:11–12

He who dwells in the shelter of the Most High
*   will rest in the shadow of the Almighty.*
I will say of the LORD, "He is my refuge and my
*   fortress,*
*   my God, in whom I trust."*

Psalm 91:1–2

If we hang around with friends who play sports (or do anything competitively) long enough, we'll hear a lot of boasting.

All over the sports scene, we hear athletes making bold claims about their dominance over others. But what would you think if someone proclaimed, "I am the weakest!" Well, that's pretty much what Paul was declaring when he told the Corinthian church about the difficulties he had encountered (see 2 Corinthians 11:16–30; 12:9). As he detailed bad event after bad event—from stonings to shipwrecks to beatings—Paul laid bare his own deficiencies. He was open about being hungry and thirsty and cold.

So why did he boast about such disheartening stuff? Why did he talk about all this anti-hero stuff? Because he wanted to tell the people of Corinth that it was okay to be on the downside of trouble, because in those kinds of circumstances we have only one source of strength.

When you're shipwrecked, you have only God to give you hope.

When you're being beaten, only God can help you survive.

When you're without resources, only God can come through as your provider.

Only when you are weak can you experience God's strength.

It's okay to cry out, "I'm the weakest." Because then you can turn to God. He is the strongest, and he will turn your weakness into a triumph of his strength.

Sports Devotional Bible

Sources

Akers, Michelle, et al. *The Sports Devotional Bible*. Grand Rapids, MI: Zondervan, 2002.

Campolo, Tony, et al. *The Teen Devotional Bible*. Grand Rapids, MI: Zondervan, 1999.

Powers, Margaret Fishback. *The Footprints Book of Prayers*. ©1996 by Margaret Fishback Powers. New York: Harper-Collins, 1996. *Life's Little Inspiration Book*. © 1995. *Life's Little Inspiration Book II*. © 1996. Footprints © 1996.

At Inspirio we love to hear from you—
your stories, your feedback,
and your product ideas.
Please send your comments to us
by way of e-mail at
icares@zondervan.com
or to the address below:

inspirio

Attn: Inspirio Cares
5300 Patterson Avenue SE
Grand Rapids, MI 49530

If you would like further information
about Inspirio and the products we
create please visit us at:
www.inspiriogifts.com

Thank you and God Bless!